S0-BED-955

A House Is a Home

by William Bernard
illustrated by Suzanne Mogensen

Harcourt
SCHOOL PUBLISHERS

Copyright © by Harcourt, Inc.

All rights reserved. No part of this publication may be reproduced or transmitted in any form or by any means, electronic or mechanical, including photocopy, recording, or any information storage and retrieval system, without permission in writing from the publisher.

Requests for permission to make copies of any part of the work should be addressed to School Permissions and Copyrights, Harcourt, Inc., 6277 Sea Harbor Drive, Orlando, Florida 32887-6777. Fax: 407-345-2418.

HARCOURT and the Harcourt Logo are trademarks of Harcourt, Inc., registered in the United States of America and/or other jurisdictions.

Printed in China

ISBN 10: 0-15-351520-1
ISBN 13: 978-0-15-351520-0

Ordering Options
ISBN 10: 0-15-351214-8 (Grade 4 Advanced Collection)
ISBN 13: 978-0-15-351214-8 (Grade 4 Advanced Collection)
ISBN 10: 0-15-358110-7 (package of 5)
ISBN 13: 978-0-15-358110-6 (package of 5)

If you have received these materials as examination copies free of charge, Harcourt School Publishers retains title to the materials and they may not be resold. Resale of examination copies is strictly prohibited and is illegal.

Possession of this publication in print format does not entitle users to convert this publication, or any portion of it, into electronic format.

3 4 5 6 7 8 9 10 985 12 11 10 09 08

Characters

Narrator	Paul's father	Paul	Katie's mother
Katie	Paul's mother	Katie's father	

Setting: An old house

Narrator: Late afternoon sun sparkles through the windows of the almost empty room. There is only a dresser and a mattress on the floor, and no curtains on the windows. In the center of the room, there are some packing boxes. Paul solemnly sits on one box, eyes downcast. Paul's mother enters.

Paul's mother: How's it going? Come on, I'll help you unpack. We can get a lot done before tonight. Then you'll feel right at home.

Narrator: Paul's mother opens a box. She takes out some clothes and puts them in one of the drawers in the dresser.

Paul: The only thing that would make me feel right at home would be to go back to our old home.

3

Narrator: Paul averts his eyes from his mother's sympathetic look.

Paul's mother: Paul, we did extensive research before picking this particular area. Everyone says it's a wonderful place to live. Then there's this house—it's over a hundred years old. Isn't that amazing?

Paul: It's just a hundred-year-old pile of wood. It's not a home. We left our home two states ago.

Paul's mother: I know you're sad, but just give it a chance. Soon you'll grow to love it just as much as our old house. Look at this big beautiful tree right out here, and see all the light coming from this window.

Paul: It's not as big as my other room.

Narrator: Paul's father is calling his mother from the kitchen.

Paul's father: Honey, where are the plates?

Paul's mother: I'll be right there! Your father wants to test his culinary skills by cooking something on the grill. Will you be okay?

Paul: I will. Don't worry, Mom.

Narrator: Paul's mother hugs him and leaves. Paul walks around the room. He pauses to peer out each window. As he walks toward the boxes, he trips over something. Paul mutters to himself.

Paul: Terrible old house.

Narrator: He looks down and sees that a floorboard has popped up slightly. Paul sits down and tugs on it. A piece of wood pops free. Paul reaches down into it and pulls out a metal box.

Paul: Treasure!

Narrator: He pries open the box and pulls out a square wrapped in a cloth. He unwraps the cloth to find a book. Paul reads the words on the first page.

Paul: *The Diary of the Legendary, Someday Famous Katie T. Jones.*

Narrator: Paul begins to read out loud.

Paul: *June 19, 1908. Dear Diary: We have just moved into our new house, so I thought it was the perfect time for a brand-new diary. I hope I have lots of things to tell you about my new life here. First, I cannot find words to describe how much I love our new house!*

Narrator: Katie, age ten, runs into the room. She wears a dress and lace-up boots from the early 1900s. She is followed by her father, who is also wearing a suit appropriate for a century ago. Katie gapes at the room, stunned by its size.

Katie: Papa, I absolutely love it!

Katie's father: I can tell.

Katie: It's huge! I never dreamed I'd ever have my own room! I've never even known anyone who had her own room.

Katie's father: Aren't you going to feel deprived, missing out on whispering and laughing all night with your sisters?

Katie: No, and I certainly won't miss listening to them toss around. I won't miss our crowded, tiny apartment at all. Goodness, this room is huge—and it's all mine!

Katie's father: We'll have to put a bell on you so you don't get lost in it. Now let's go help your mother. She's feeling a little queasy in this heat.

Narrator: They leave. Paul closes the diary and sits pensively for a moment, looking around the room.

Narrator: It's the next morning. Paul trudges into the kitchen, where Mom and Dad are sitting at the table eating breakfast. Paul sits down at the table.

Paul's father: Hey, there, how did you like your first night in your new room?

Paul: I didn't get any sleep. The branches on that big old tree kept tapping on the window. It was creepy.

Paul's mother: You won't even notice it in a few days. It's such a lovely old maple tree—it was young when this house was built.

Paul: I just think it's annoying.

Paul's father: I'm driving out to the garden store to pick up some things. Do you want to come with me?

Paul: No, thanks—I found this diary in my room. I really want to read it.

Narrator: Paul sits outside on the front steps, reading the diary. The big maple tree is next to the house.

Paul: *June 30, 1908. Dear Diary: There is a young maple tree next to the house. I wish it were tall enough to reach my window. Then I could touch the leaves and make friends with the birds that sit on its branches. I wonder how many years it will take to get that tall?*

Narrator: Katie walks across the yard and sits serenely beneath the small tree, looking blissfully at the leaves.

Katie: When you look up, all you see is green. It's no longer leaves on a tree, but a new kind of vivid green sky.

Narrator: Paul sits down next to her and also looks up.

Paul: I think I know what you mean.

Narrator: Paul is in his room. The windows now have curtains and some of the boxes are gone. Paul sits on the bed, reading the diary. Paul's father pokes his head in the door.

Paul's father: Hey, kid, can I recruit you to help me out with something in the garden?

Paul: Sure—I'll be right there, Dad.

Paul's father: That diary must be really interesting. Anyway, whenever you're ready.

Narrator: Paul's father leaves, and Paul reads from the diary.

Paul: *August 5, 1908. The summer is passing so quickly! Every day there is something new to do. I've been exploring on my pony, Scout. Yesterday I found a patch of wild strawberries. I'm going to go back today to pick some.*

Narrator: Katie, wearing an old-fashioned bathing dress, runs to the front of the house.

Katie: Mama, I'm going swimming in the creek with Ellen and Cynthia Franklin and their mother!

Narrator: Katie's mother walks out the door and onto the front porch. She smiles at Katie.

Katie's mother: All right, but don't wear yourself out. I'm going to need your help if you want strawberry ice cream tonight.

Katie: With my strawberries? Of course I can help. I'm strong—I can turn the crank on the ice cream maker for hours!

Katie's mother: Well, I hope it won't take that long! Maybe we can take some over to the Franklins later tonight.

Katie: All right—I won't tell them. It'll be a surprise! See you later!

Paul: *August 22, 1908. Dear Diary—To my consternation, summer is almost over, and school will soon commence. I'm looking forward to making new friends, but I'll miss all the lazy days I've spent here.*

Narrator: Katie and her father are outside. She runs over to the tree and puts her arms around it.

Katie: I have an idea—can you put a swing on this tree?

Katie's father: I don't think so, Katie. It's still a young tree. The branches aren't strong enough, but maybe in a year or two we can.

Katie: I can't wait. Then everything will be just about perfect.

Narrator: Paul's mother scrapes the wall of his room with a paint scraper, as Paul looks on curiously.

Paul's mother: We'll go to the paint store, and you can pick out any color you want. There are lots of layers of old paint that we'll need to strip off, though. There! I think this blue is the bottom of it.

Paul: Do you mean that's the original color from when this house was first built?

Paul's mother: Probably.

Paul: Then that's the color I want, something reminiscent of how it used to look.

Paul's mother: I thought you didn't care about this "hundred-year-old pile of wood."

Paul: I was wrong. It's not just a pile of wood. It's not even just a building. It's a place where people lived and thought and played. There were birthdays and holidays and summer days and winter nights here, all belonging to real people. All of that history is here in this house. I want to be part of it, too.

Paul's mother: I know what you mean. We'll add our own memories. Now let's go to the store and try to match this color.

Paul: All right. Mom—do you think we could put a swing on that tree out there?

Think Critically

1. Why is Paul unhappy in the first scene?

2. How are Katie's and Paul's reactions to the house different?

3. How does reading Katie's diary affect Paul?

4. Why does Paul want to paint his room the same as the original color?

5. How would you feel if you were Paul and had moved into the old house?

 Art

Dream House Draw a picture of your dream house. Then write a paragraph that describes the house and explains your choices.

School-Home Connection Choose a few pages from this Readers' Theater. Read them aloud with a family member or a friend. Don't forget to speak clearly and with feeling!

Word Count: 1,497